Marine Birds
FROM THE NORTHEAST COAST

Enjoy bird watching at the beach!
Joanne Roach-Evans

WRITTEN AND ILLUSTRATED BY
J. ROACH-EVANS

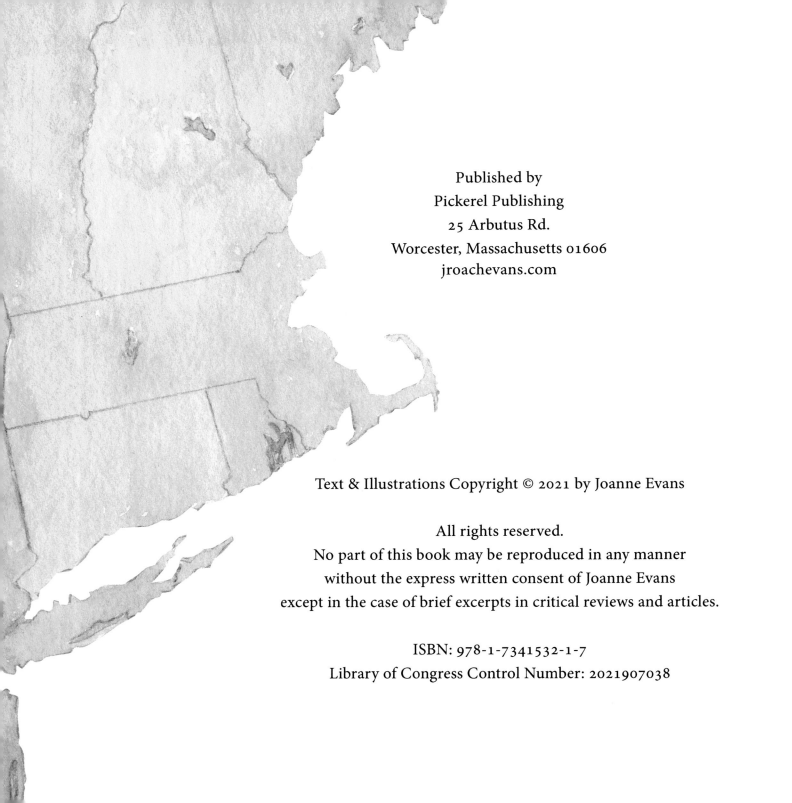

Published by
Pickerel Publishing
25 Arbutus Rd.
Worcester, Massachusetts 01606
jroachevans.com

ISBN: 978-1-7341532-1-7
Library of Congress Control Number: 2021907038

for the Mungovan boys

Patrick John & Michael

with love

There are birds of the field,
and birds of the wood,
and birds

that belong to the sea
and its shore.

If there is one bird
that you may think of
when you think
of the sea,

it is the bird
that you most often see.

Can you guess what it is?

It is the **seagull** of course!
It even has the "sea" in its name.
Most people call these birds seagulls because
they are often located by the sea.

In fact, they are just called "gulls" officially!
Each gull is given their own name.
This type of gull is a **herring gull**.
This adult herring gull
has a red mark under its beak,
yellow eyes, and pink legs and feet.

Herring gulls are quite common - you may even see them
away from the coast.

grey feathers on their
back and wings

white and black
tail feathers

pink legs

The **ring-billed** gull is also seen
just about everywhere.
Can you see the ring of black around its beak?
That is where it got its name!

For the first few years of their lives,
both the **herring gull** and the **ring-billed gull**
have a mix of white and
grey or black feathers on their heads.
When they are adults, they will have white
feathered heads.

The ring-billed gull
has yellow eyes and
yellow legs.

grey feathers on their
back and wings

yellow legs

white and black
tail feathers

white and black tail feathers

pink legs

One of the biggest gulls of all is called the
great black-backed gull.

This adult gull has a red mark on its beak,
and pink legs like the herring gull.
How can you tell them apart?

The great black-backed gull
is the biggest gull on the beach.

They have dark black feathers
on their backs and wings.

But watch out for gulls because
they are scavengers and all
scavengers are known to do the
same thing...

They will steal your food!

Because scavengers will eat just about anything,
they will even eat your sandwich!

Although they can eat almost anything, they are
much healthier when they eat their natural foods
like insects, fish, crabs, and clams.

Common terns have orange beaks and feet.

Smaller seabirds that are related to the gulls are the **terns.**
They are often seen flying over the water
using their excellent eyesight to find little fish to eat.
Terns dive headfirst from high in the sky, plunging into the ocean
to catch fish underwater in their beaks!

These terns are called
common terns and **least terns.**
They both have black feather caps.

The least terns can look like little bandits
with their black masks,
but don't worry, they won't steal your sandwich!

*Least terns have yellow
beaks and feet.*

In springtime terns nest right on the beach.
You sometimes see them flying back to their nest
where they may have eggs or chicks to feed and protect.

AREA
CLOSED
THREATENED BIRDS NESTING

LEAST TERN   COMMON TERN   PIPING PLOVER

If birds are disturbed parents may leave the nest,
subjecting eggs and young to exposure and possible death.
ENTERING AREA VIOLATION OF STATE AND FEDERAL LAW.

Shorebirds called **piping plovers**
make their nests on the sand too.
They do not dive for fish, but instead search the seashore
for tasty things to eat.

A close relative of the piping plovers
are the **semi-palmated plovers.**

You can tell the difference between the two
by the darker feathers, white neck collars, and
black breast bands of the semi-palmated plovers.

You may see piping plovers
and semi-palmated plovers
with other small shorebirds,
like sanderlings,
at the water's edge.
They are all about the same size
and forage by running, stopping, and
pecking the sand for prey.

Sanderlings

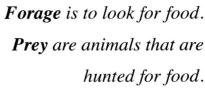

Forage *is to look for food.*
Prey *are animals that are*
hunted for food.

Sanderlings are another common shorebird.

They are fun to watch as they run back and forth with the waves.

Sanderlings have pale feathers and longer beaks than the plovers.
They use their long beaks to probe the sand for food like little mole
crabs and marine worms. Sanderlings are in the sandpiper family.

A relative of the sanderling is the **purple sandpiper**.

You may not see them on the sandy beach,

but, if you're up on a jetty,

you may see them looking for food around the rocks.

They eat many things
that live on the rocks and in the seaweed -
like periwinkles, small crabs, and the seaweed itself.

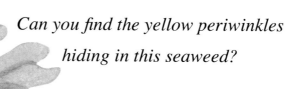

Can you find the yellow periwinkles
hiding in this seaweed?

Out on the rocks and on the water you can see the big, black **double-crested cormorants**. It's fun to watch them diving for fish, crabs, and other marine creatures.

Cormorants can dive underwater for more than a minute!

When they are done diving,
they find a place to stand and open their wings
to dry out their wet feathers.

Out on the water along a rocky shore, you might see a large
and beautiful sea duck called a **common eider**.
Eiders are the largest ducks
on the North American coast.

They can dive deep down in the ocean
to catch mussels, crabs, and sea urchins hiding in the rocks.
They can dive up to 65 feet! *(That's deeper than a telephone pole!)*

Like many birds, the boys are more colorful than the girls.
The male eider is striking in his black and white markings.
The female's soft brown coloring is perfect
for hiding on her nest to keep her eggs and chicks safe.

Whether marine birds spend their lives
on the open ocean,
or migrate and nest along the coast,

or if they dive for fish and crabs,
or probe the sand for worms,
some of the most remarkable birds
belong to the sea and its shore.

SEABIRDS

Gulls, Terns, & Cormorants

Herring Gull

Ring-Billed Gull

Great Black-Backed Gull

Least Tern

Common Tern

Double-Crested
Cormorant

SHOREBIRDS

Sandpipers & Plovers

Sanderling

Purple Sandpiper

Piping Plover

Semi-Palmated Plover

SEA DUCKS

Eiders

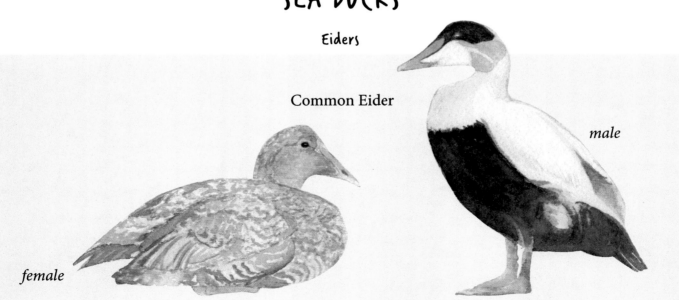

Common Eider

male

female

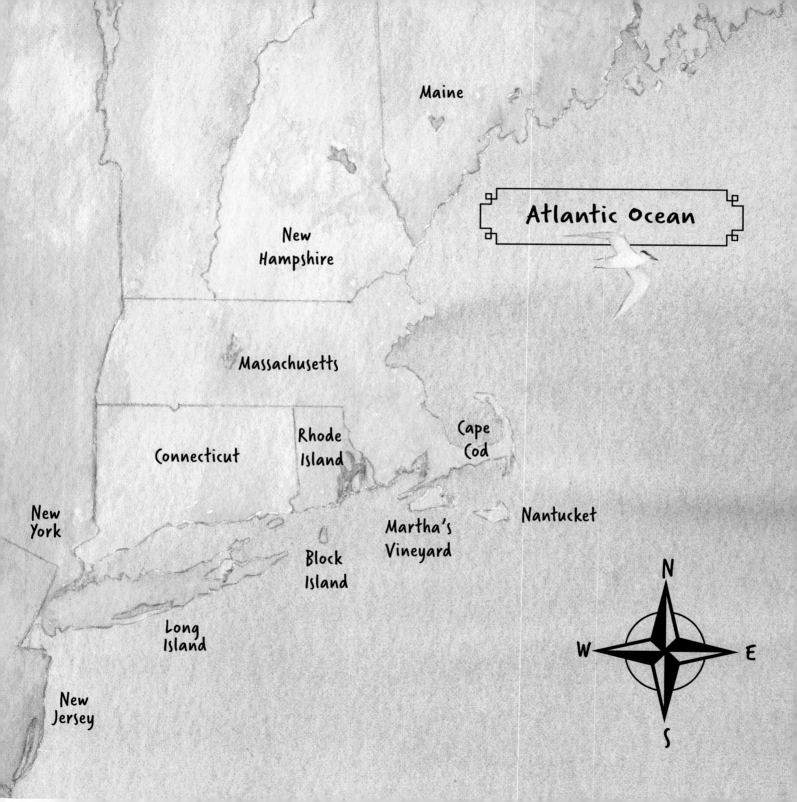

More Cool Things About Marine Birds

- Gulls are also found inland where they may live by lakes or even visit landfills and dumpsters looking for food.

- When terns dive from the air into the water to catch fish it is called "plunge diving".

- Male and female terns and plovers take turns tending their eggs and protecting their chicks, often staying with them for months while they learn to fly.

- Plovers eat worms, crabs, bugs, and snails.

- Cormorants are found all around the world. Like gulls, they can live on lakes as well as the sea.

- Most shorebirds are migratory, meaning they are just stopping by to eat or raise a family. The terns and piping plovers nest on northeast beaches in the spring and fly south for the winter. Adult sanderlings and semi-palmated plovers nest in the far north.

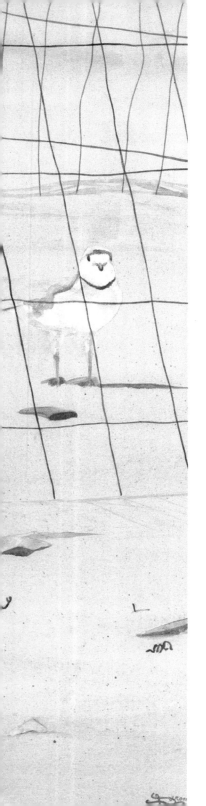

HOW YOU CAN HELP MARINE BIRDS

• Piping plover and tern eggs look just like sand, so they can be very difficult to see. Dogs and people have been known to step on them without even knowing. There are kind people who try to protect them by putting up temporary fencing or string around areas where they make their nests. Please give them lots of space and do not fly kites or let dogs near them. Keep an eye out for plover and tern chicks as they blend in with the sand; they cannot fly and should not be chased.

NOTE: Not all states have the same laws to protect terns and piping plovers. Some states list them as threatened and some list them as endangered.

• Do not feed seagulls and try to keep your food safely away from them. They will often swallow plastic bags in order to get the food inside. Plastic is very dangerous for all birds to swallow.

To learn more about Marine Birds
check out these great websites:

Audubon Guide to North American birds: **audubon.org**

The Cornell Lab: **allaboutbirds.org**

The Sea Duck Joint Venture: **seaduckjv.org**

You can also check out Joanne's blog & YouTube videos
@ jroachevans.com

Sanderlings

Joanne Roach-Evans is the author and illustrator of several seashore books: Seashells, Treasures from the Northeast Coast; Seaweed, Marine Algae from the Northeast Coast; Marine Animals from the Northeast Coast; and Marine Birds from the Northeast Coast. She is an avid beachcomber and a curious naturalist. Joanne has always enjoyed watching birds, whether at home in central Massachusetts or while spending time at her beloved seashore.

Author's note: I used quite a few field guides to research this book. One of my favorite books for kids would be the Smithsonian Kids' Field Guide, Birds of North America, East. So when you're ready to learn more their field guide makes a great next step!

If you like this book please leave a review on Amazon - Thank you!

Made in the USA
Middletown, DE
11 September 2021

47556664R00022